BEYOND THE WILDERNESS

Other Destiny Image Books by Thom Gardner

Growing Up Into Christ: A Study in Integrated Spiritual Formation

Healing the Wounded Heart: Removing Obstacles to Intimacy with God

The Healing Journey: An Interactive Guide to Spiritual Wholeness

Living the God-Breathed Life: An Invitation to Rest at the Table

Relentless Love: Unfolding God's Passion, Presence, and Glory

Altars of the Heart

THOM GARDNER

BEYOND THE WILDERNESS

DISCOVERING OPPORTUNITY IN CRISIS

DESTINY IMAGE® PUBLISHERS, INC.

PO Box 310, Shippensburg, PA 17257-0310

"Promoting Inspired Lives"

This book and all other Destiny Image and Destiny Image Fiction books are available at Christian bookstores and distributors worldwide.

For more information on foreign distributors, call 717-532-3040.

Or reach us on the Internet: www.destinyimage.com

ISBN 13 TP: 978-0-7684-5693-6

ISBN 13 EBook: 978-0-7684-5694-3

For Worldwide Distribution.

1 2 3 4 5 6 / 23 22 21 20

Contents

Chapter 1

Hidden Treasure Under Our Feet

> *I will give you the treasures of darkness and hidden wealth of secret places, that you may know that it is I, The LORD, the God of Israel, who calls you by your name* (Isaiah 45:3).

You and I are surrounded by hidden treasures. Consider the true story of an unnamed family, who, while walking through a flea market, purchased an old white bowl. The bowl sat on their mantle for a long while until they thought to have someone appraise its value. To their shock and delight, they discovered the seemingly plain bowl was worth a considerable amount. It later sold for $2.2 million at auction. There it had been on the mantle all along right in front of them. Another man discovered that behind a plain picture frame was a copy of the Declaration of Independence commissioned by John Quincy Adams in 1820. Again, priceless.

At the moment of this writing, our nation is engulfed in a pandemic affecting millions of people with great sickness, death, and economic catastrophe. Our ministry has fielded the calls of many individuals who feel lost in this uncharted terrain. There is no plan nor compass to guide their steps, leaving them feeling lost in a fog.

When we are in such a fog, we may ask ourselves how can we get out of this arid and untenable reality? In our wandering, we may feel fear or confusion, hopelessness. We may feel alone and overwhelmed when none of our familiar formulas for life seem to work. It feels like wilderness. How could anything good come from this? Yet there may be hidden or unmined treasure beneath our feet at this moment.

In 2010, thirty-three miners were trapped 2,300 feet below ground in a mine cave-in. To the outside world there seemed very little hope of good to come from this tragedy. Yet, God was doing something amazing as the entire world was fixed on this disaster for many days. In the midst of this crisis hidden in utter darkness, the light of Christ was shining from one humble common follower of Jesus Christ, José Henriquez. He wrote of the experience:

> As I took hold of what I had learned and began to talk to my companions about the Lord, God began to work in them and gave them an opportunity to know him and communicate with him. Some of them were immediately brought out of darkness, and with great joy I saw how the Lord was transforming their lives.[1]

There could have been no more precious treasure mined from the darkness than the light of Christ and transformed lives. The world was watching to see if or how these men might come out of the 70-day ordeal. The rescue from this particular wilderness got the attention of a fascinated world and hidden treasure came out the darkness.

Such unmined treasure may lay around us like so much junk littering the landscape to be stepped over or ignored because we don't recognize its value and potential. These treasures hold power for the healing and comfort not only for us but for others around us if we could only learn to see them. You are likely standing amid these great resources as you read these words. They are in plain sight around you even now. The treasures I'm speaking of are the brokenness, disappointments, even failures we've experienced in our times of personal wilderness past and present that may be invested with new purpose and value.

This book, which is part of a larger upcoming work, was germinated out of our formational counseling ministry for a couple of decades. Part of that ministry is to help others to recognize the value of brokenness of the past or challenges of the present to see their eternal possibilities and to infuse them with new vision and purpose. In short, to *repurpose* them.

One of the frequent questions that arise out of various kinds of traumas and challenges or loss is "Why?" Maybe we've lost a loved one or are presented with a difficult diagnosis. Perhaps we've lost a job or a marriage. The shards of our circumstances lay around us like a piece of broken pottery. We ask, "Why?" or "Why me?" We cry out, "God where are You? Where did You go?"

We may believe that God has abandoned us or that we've somehow gone out of reach of His tender love and care. "Why, God?" We may question our identity and security in the love of God. Beloved, God has not moved. He has not changed His mind about us. Our identity as His beloved has not changed. A loving embrace awaits us in the healing arms of Jesus to resolve the lies ingested because of trauma and challenges.

But there is more—much more. God repurposes our flops, failures, and wounds to bring further healing to us and to establish His presence in and through us. The apostle Paul writes, *"I am of the opinion that there is no comparison between the pain of this present time and the glory which we will see in the future"* (Romans 8:18 Bible in Basic English).

It is my prayer that the following chapters may be a map or a compass out of the wilderness to help us find unexpected gold of our past trauma or present grief—to find a new vision and hope for the present and future. We will ask a few questions along the way, including:

- What does it mean to repurpose our lives?
- How do we learn to see with a new vision?

In this writing, we will define and explore the repurposing of our lives. As we present our broken pieces to the feet of the Great Repurposer, they will be transformed and infused with new purpose and power to bring release from captivity, passage through seemingly insurmountable obstacles, refreshing in the wilderness, and victory over the enemy of discouragement. More than anything else, our repurposed lives will become evidence of the amazing and *repurposing grace* of God.

The following chapters reveal the repurposing grace of God in the lives of ordinary and imperfect people just like us. There are a few stories from real people along the road of their journey who found the hidden treasure, even in the wilderness. We will take inventory of our own lives and see foundations for hope filled with new possibilities as we find *A Life Repurposed*. Each subsequent chapter includes an opportunity to reflect on your own life to find the hidden treasure waiting to be repurposed in the hand of God. We refer to this as *The Turn Around*.

I hope that a conversation will begin though these pages between you and the One who repurposes what you place at His feet. God is the Great Repurposer—the Craftsman of creation itself. Listen as He says to you, *"Behold, I am making all things new"* (Revelation 21:5).

The Turn Around

Are there thoughts or memories of past challenges or preoccupations with present circumstances that rise to the surface from time to time like a beach ball in a swimming pool? Do you push them down under the water only to have them pop up again? Perhaps you've underestimated them. Take a few minutes and reflect on these buoyant thoughts and experiences. You may want to note a few of them on the lines that follow here or in your journal.

Note

1. Jose Henriquez, *Miracle in the Mine: One Man's Story of Strength and Survival in the Chilean Mines* (Grand Rapids, MI: Zondervan, 2011), 67-68.

Chapter 2

Life Repurposed

Many years ago when I was in college as a music education major, I took classes at two different campuses: Saint Vincent College in Latrobe and Seton Hill College in Greensburg, Pennsylvania. I commuted between campuses driving along a back-country road along green rolling hills with a house here and a farm there along the way. I threw my trumpet case and books in the back seat of my white Karman Ghia convertible and breathed in the fresh air with the top down (weather permitting, of course). The drive and scenery provided a little decompression and refreshment between classes and rehearsals.

On one of those days, I observed a spot along the route where someone had begun to pile up what looked like junk; a piece of lumber here, a window there, maybe a door or other odd building materials lying about. As months rolled by, I would occasionally see a middle-aged man dressed in an unexceptional way, steadily pushing a construction wheelbarrow filled with more junk up the hill or perhaps cleaning the mortar off old bricks or just organizing his heaps of what appeared to be junk.

He was assembling older, used building materials from who knows where—a demolished house or office building perhaps. There were windows and doors and pieces of metal, wood framing lumber. I'm sure he had to buy some new things, but basically he gathered building materials that apparently people didn't see as having much value or potential. The materials piled up over some time to become quite a collection. I recall feeling a little resentful of this man and his ad hoc junkyard. It was a real eyesore along an otherwise green and peaceful road. This irreverent treatment of the landscape lasted for many months, maybe a year.

I can't recall the total amount of time that elapsed, but what seemed like a random junkyard began to take on definite shape and purpose. One of those days on my drive, to my great surprise, a foundation for a small house emerged from the ground. As I watched over some time, recycled bricks became walls. Discarded doors and windows were refinished and installed to fit perfectly into what emerged from the heap to become a place to live!

That house still stands these many years later. The builder took what seemed to be a useless heap of cast-off debris and *repurposed* it to become a habitation. This anonymous man's house of repurposed materials could be a metaphor for life as well. The house is still there with a new owner. His repurposed house lives on.

What Is Repurposing?

It has become popular to *repurpose* items ranging from old furniture to picture frames, to farm tools and any number of other items. I once had dinner in a restaurant in Erie, Pennsylvania, where the entrepreneur repurposed an old railroad passenger car to become the dining room. There have been entire TV programs devoted to refurbishing and decorating homes with repurposed pieces.

We live close to Pennsylvania Dutch country where it is not unusual to see somebody repurpose an old plow or some farm implement to become the centerpiece of their landscape surrounded by flowers and new life. Some visionary builders may use repurposed or reclaimed lumber from a dilapidated barn to build new furniture or decorate an accent wall of a new home. Not only are these repurposed pieces environmentally responsible, but they also bring character and depth to their new environment. My wife and I have a few repurposed pieces in our home.

To be repurposed is to see obsolete or unused items with a new vision and to infuse them with new life and adapt them to a new purpose. To repurpose disregarded resources requires imagination and artistry to see them with potential beyond the way they may have originally been conceived.

My wife, Carol, is a drama and English teacher. One of the productions she organized was of *The Lion, the Witch, and the Wardrobe* by C.S. Lewis. In her dramatic productions, Carol demonstrated the ability to see potential in items that others may not always see. In the production of the C.S. Lewis classic, Carol needed a large crown to adorn the head of the White Witch, but couldn't find one that fit this important character in the play. Then, while walking through a particular retail shop, she saw a wire wastebasket with the approximate dimension of the crown she envisioned on the brow of this sinister character. The bottom was removed and the rim lined and the whole piece was painted white. Where others saw a wastebasket, Carol saw a perfect crown.

My dad was another person who was a good *repurposer.* He had a great passion to adapt and repurpose old furniture or disregarded mechanical parts in his workshop. For instance, Dad repurposed baby food jars to hold an assortment of nuts and bolts and other bits of hardware and mounted them on wooden disks suspended from the ceiling on a spindle. Once, an electric motor from a discarded appliance was fixed to a flexible cable to become a sanding wheel. In all of the cases above, supposed obsolete artifacts were enlisted to new vision, purpose, and value-adding depth and beauty to those who repurposed them.

God the Creator and Re-creator

The following verses describe God's self-disclosed repertoire of repurposing craftsmanship.

> *That men may know from the rising to the setting of the sun that there is no one besides Me. I am the LORD, and there is no other, the One **forming** light and **creating** darkness, causing well-being and creating calamity; I am the LORD who does all these* (Isaiah 45:6-7).

The keywords and images here are "*forming*" and "*creating.*" Both words describe something fashioned in the hand of the Craftsman of creation. Forming refers to something reshaped from existing material, while creating implies the bringing forth of something out of nothing. God does both. God forms and reshapes even the darkness to His purpose.

When we look at the context of the Scripture from Isaiah 45, it is clear that Isaiah was talking about a pagan king, Cyrus, who would not be born for many years after Isaiah's prophetic word. Cyrus would be repurposed to return the people of God to the ruined city of Jerusalem.

> *Thus says Cyrus king of Persia, "The LORD, the God of heaven, has given me all the kingdoms of the earth and He has appointed me to build Him a house in Jerusalem, which is in Judah. Whoever there is among you of all His people, may his God be with him!*

> *Let him go up to Jerusalem which is in Judah and rebuild the house of the LORD, the God of Israel; He is the God who is in Jerusalem"* (Ezra 1:2-3).

The LORD, the God of Heaven called this conquering king to transform a heap into a habitation for God and His people. Truly there is no God besides the LORD. God's creativity or re-creativity is boundless. It is who God is. His heart and creative nature are seen through every means we can imagine, even what looks to us like devastation.

A few years ago, Carol and I were in a forested area at the foothills of the Blue Mountains in New South Wales, Australia. There had been a terrible forest fire that had been reported in the media even as far away as the United States. We had visited the region many times and were interested to see the results of that devastating blaze. A friend knowledgeable in the things of nature drove us into the burned forest to observe the devastating result of the fire.

We were astonished to see what I thought was a species of tree that we had never seen. The forest was filled with trees that had blackened bark but was also surrounded by fresh, green life. I inquired, "What kind of tree is this with black bark and such green leaves?" My friend then unveiled the grand refreshing and repurposing work of God through nature, even fire. There were seeds pods on the bark of the trees that were broken open by the fire, spewing out seeds for new growth. The result was an amazing and surreal contrast of the black bark from the devastation of fire against the delicate green of fresh life. Because God can repurpose a fire to bring new life out of devastation, what else might we place at His feet?

God repurposes all the good, the bad, and the ugly as we release our lives into His hands in Christ. The apostle Paul, himself a repurposed persecutor of the church, writes, "*Now we look inside, and what we see is that anyone united with the Messiah gets a fresh start, is created new. The old life is gone; a new life burgeons!*" (2 Corinthians 5:17 The Message). In Christ we aren't just getting a new paint job—not a mere cosmetic makeover. In God's recreative hand we are converted into something brand-new—new nature, new identity, a new purpose.

It is important to know that as our past challenges or present circumstances are repurposed, we are not talking about renovation or remodeling. Something new is coming forth in the hand of God. Everyone who belongs to Christ, who has put their lives with all of the challenges or griefs or failures at His disposal is becoming brand-new.

God sees potential we don't see.

God, the Artist and Craftsman of creation and recreation, often rummages through the broken and disregarded pieces of our lives to repurpose them into something that will bring Him glory. He sees something in our wanderings that we may not see. We have all faced, or may be facing now, various kinds of challenges along life's road. We may see them as I saw what appeared to be a heap of junk along my drive those years ago. We may have written them off as an interruption to spoil the scenery of our journey. But these repurposed pieces teach us. They soften us. They speak to us and through us of God's repurposing grace.

In our ministry, we have often used pieces of a Japanese art form called *kintsugi* to illustrate the value of repurposing. Hundreds of years ago a powerful Japanese emperor entrusted a precious broken vessel to a craftsman for repair. He chose a unique adhesive to reconstruct the vessel. The broken shards were put together with gold. Now, what began as a piece of pottery, became a far more precious work of art. So the Craftsman of Heaven often puts our broken pieces together with the gold of His repurposing grace, making us new creations in Christ.

As we journey with God, we need to think about our challenges differently. Might God have a purpose beyond healing? Can we place cancer or some other serious illness at His disposal? Can a traumatic event become an open doorway to redirect our lives? We must move beyond an explanation of suffering where we ask "Why?" and into asking, "What's next?" The shift happens as we find the heart and presence of God rather than what He might do for us. It is a shift toward maturity.

When we first come to Christ we are interested in what God might do for us. But as we mature in that relationship, we become more devoted to the Person and purpose of God and less focused on what He might do for us.

As Tim Clinton writes:

> When we come to know God, we do so with the same selfish hang-ups we had before believing. But it's the Holy Spirit's working in our hearts and lives that ultimately removes the selfish

> motives and desires to move us toward a deeper relationship with him—one that is more focused on serving him, not ourselves.[1]

It is possible that our scars can become a road map for another person's healing. When Jesus showed Himself to His followers after the resurrection, He showed them His scars that were now being repurposed to demonstrate His love and grace. The Bible recounts a repurposing of the passion of Christ from fear and despair to joy.

> *So when it was evening on that day, the first day of the week, and when the doors were shut where the disciples were, for fear of the Jews, Jesus came and stood in their midst and said to them, "Peace be with you." And when He had said this, He showed them both His hands and His side. The disciples*

> *then rejoiced when they saw the Lord* (John 20:19-20).

Our repurposed scars draw us closer to God. Again Clinton writes:

> ...God doesn't wipe away our past; instead, he uses every element of it—the wonderful, the horrible, and the senseless—to weave a new, beautiful, strong fabric of our lives. We may remember these events for the rest of our lives, but they won't threaten or control us any longer. We'll be deeply grateful that God used them—even them—to teach us life's richest lessons and draw us closer to him.[2]

Revelation 21:5 says, *"Behold, I make all things new."* When the word "behold" is used in the Scriptures, it generally means something new is about to be released. New vision. New depth of relationship with God.

In our ministry of formational counseling and spiritual direction, we have sought to bring people to an understanding of who they truly are in Christ. Part of that ministry is to help those to whom we minister to take inventory of all the steps that led up to their present season and show them that God can redeem and repurpose even the worst trauma. Whatever the issue, we have come to know that God is a repurposing God who turns trauma into triumph, failure into freedom, and pain into power.

Though our beloved friends found healing and peace, there often remained a question about what God might do with the debris field that lay behind them. How would someone who experienced a great loss or wounding possibly bring something positive out of their experience? This repurposing, in fact, is part of the continuing unfolding of the artistry and presence of God in our lives.

God is a *repurposing* God who infuses new purpose in the artifacts of our journey resurrected from the sands of our wandering through our times of wilderness. Like the man with the house of repurposed building materials, our heaps of challenges and disappointments can become a habitation for the presence of God. What is needed is that we choose to see them as potential building materials for the Kingdom of God and release them to His feet for transformation and new purpose, where grief can become compassion for another's loss; where trauma and disappointment can bring new life; where a challenging diagnosis might become a new mission field—*"so that we will be able to comfort those who are in any affliction with the comfort with which we ourselves are comforted by God"* (2 Corinthians 1:4).

Let us now be open to seeing our lives with new eyes of hope and potential.

> *God can do anything, you know—far more than you could ever imagine or guess or request in your wildest dreams! He does it not by pushing us around but by working within us, his Spirit deeply and gently within us* (Ephesians 3:20 The Message).

The Turn Around

Our journey is filled with transitions and broken pieces. Let's take time to inventory some of those broken pieces to see what the Great Artist and Craftsman of creation might do with them. In your own experience, what has God already repurposed in your life? This is an invitation to see what God sees. Make a list of what comes to mind. We will watch to see how God might repurpose these to the benefit of His people including you. Start your inventory with praise, reading and reflecting on the following verse:

> *You have turned my mourning into joyful dancing. You have taken away my clothes of mourning and clothed me with joy, that I might sing praises to you and not be silent. O LORD my God, I will give you thanks forever!* (Psalm 30:11-12 New Living Translation)

Notes

1. Tim Clinton, *God Attachment: Why You Believe, Act, and Feel the Way You Do About God* (Howard Books; Kindle Edition, 2010), loc. 895.

2. Ibid.

Chapter 3

Pick-Up Sticks

> *Therefore, behold, I will allure her, and bring her into the wilderness, and speak to her heart to her* (Hosea 2:14, author's translation).

A few years back I was sitting at my computer reflecting on the goodness of God and all of the blessings He had opened up in every realm of my life. My kids were doing well, and I was experiencing increased opportunities to speak into the lives of many hurting people, seeing them grow personally. God is good! In the middle of the voice of triumph, I opened a new file to begin a new manuscript.

Just as the goodness of God was overwhelming and erupting from my heart, another voice began to vie for my attention from some deep and dark place. At first it was a faint thought, but the voice grew louder as I gave it space. This voice intruded into my peace whispering, "Who do you think you are? You know the mess that's been in your life. Who do you think you are to minister to anyone or to write books about God. You are a mess, a flop, a failure. Who do you think you are!?"

I was caught off balance—flatfooted, and did not know what to do with the question. Then I asked myself, "Who do I think I am?" The words and the question were familiar to me. I have, at times, been a model of mediocrity and self-centeredness. Having allowed my heart to attend these self-defeating thoughts, I simply deferred the question to the One who knows the answer: "Lord, who do You think I am?" Then a concert of silence. Nevertheless, the question continued, "Lord, who do You think I am?"

A little later while I was sitting in the lounge of a repair garage having my car serviced, I sensed the Lord saying, "I'm ready to answer your question now." The next moment brought an unexpected reply as my mind held an image of a child's game, Pick-Up Sticks. This image puzzled me as

I hadn't thought about that game for many decades. How did this image of a kid's game answer my question? "Lord, who do You think I am?"

Pick-Up Sticks is played by dropping the bundle of brightly colored wooden or plastic "sticks" onto the floor or the top of a table resulting in what looks like a miniature, multicolored logjam, then moving the sticks one at a time from the pile using one black stick called the master stick. The score is calculated by the number and color of sticks moved without disturbing the other sticks. The sticks are moved using the master stick. I seldom played the game and was never very good at it when I did.

The more I thought about it, the clearer the meaning became. At times, my life, with all of its imperfections, reminds me of that little disheveled pile of sticks. The sticks are my many failings or challenges past and present, or maybe facets of my life that seem random and trivial. There are times when I hear God's invitation to greater intimacy or to join in what He may be doing; but instead of responding and moving ahead in God, I turn around and look at the little logjam behind me. I add up the score of the dropped sticks and consider myself the loser and disqualified. Then I'm stuck. I have to wonder how there could be any purpose in this pile of sticks—anything redeemable.

As I pondered the image of pick-up sticks, the Lord reminded me of another man with a few "sticks" in his life—Moses. Moses had an encounter with God on holy ground, a man who had received instruction from the personal presence of God. Eventually, Moses would lead thousands of God's people out of bondage, go through seemingly impossible obstacles, battle the enemies of God, and bring water out of a rock to a thirsty people. But before the power and glory, there was a wilderness.

The Wilderness Is Wild

> *Now Moses was pasturing the flock of Jethro his father-in-law, the priest of Midian; and he led the flock to the west side of the* ***wilderness*** *and came to Horeb, the mountain of God* (Exodus 3:1).

The key to our English *wilderness* word is *wild.* A wilderness is a wild or uncultivated place where we don't know the rules—where there is no map or GPS to get us around. There are many kinds of wilderness, from financial wilderness to cultural wilderness. We may find ourselves in a wilderness of a medical waiting room waiting to hear test results for ourselves or a loved one. Maybe we find ourselves in a wilderness of financial crisis or career loss. The wilderness can be growing older, sitting on the frontier of retirement. Grief can also be a wilderness. On grief, Alan Wolfet writes:

> Think of your grief as a wilderness—a vast, mountainous, inhospitable forest. You are in the wilderness now. You are in the midst of unfamiliar and often brutal surroundings. You are cold and tired. Yet you must journey through this wilderness. To find your way out, you must become acquainted with its terrain and learn to follow the sometimes hard-to-find trail that leads to healing.[1]

Our personal wilderness seems to lack life or potential, causing us to give in to doubt or discouragement and feelings of being alone in the face of the formidable, unfamiliar, and untamed landscape before us.

Bill's Wilderness

Bill was a man in his late middle age who had worked the same stable and predictable job for more than twenty years. The large company Bill worked for was shifting people into new positions to keep up with the changing times and technology. After his many years of service, Bill's supervisor informed him that he would be changing positions and roles within the organization. While Bill was assured that he would still have a good position within the company, he immediately felt uneasy. Change was not Bill's best friend. Change became Bill's wilderness and it caused him tremendous anxiety. He felt alone and unsure of what lay ahead.

The first day at his new position Bill crossed the threshold of a new building seeing unfamiliar faces and was led to a work station where he would perform a job he was not yet trained for. He experienced a panic attack and had to leave the facility. Bill was in a wilderness. Later, Bill was referred to our ministry for counseling where we spent time looking at the source on his anxiety. As we prayed and talked, we found that his anxiety stemmed from an experience early in his life coming from a critical family and a particularly difficult time with a school teacher.

Bill was able to find truth and healing as he acknowledged his fear in the presence of the Lord and forgave the offenses that led to his anxiety. In effect, we had to reenter the wilderness of Bill's childhood and find God in the midst of it. Bill returned to work and engaged in his new position. In Bill's case, his wilderness required healing of an ungodly belief resulting in preparation for a whole new chapter of life.

There is a difference between a desert and the wilderness. Wilderness is a place or condition where there are still resources. You might think, for instance, of Jesus being in a place where He fed 5,000 and another 4,000 people as told in the Gospels. Our greatest resource in the wilderness is the Spirit of God. The wilderness, of whatever kind, can be unfamiliar and may seem lonely. However, the wilderness is also a season of listening to God, of separation and preparation. The Bible is filled with examples of individuals who experienced the wilderness and God used that time to their benefit and to fulfill His purpose.

The Wilderness Is a Place of Separation

I once heard a precious sister say, "I'm not sure where I'm going, but I'm sure I'll get there." In the wilderness, of whatever kind, the paths are unfamiliar. Most of the people who amounted to anything in the Bible of human existence went through times of wilderness. Consider Abraham, the friend of God. *"By faith Abraham, when he was called, obeyed by going out to a place which he was to receive for an inheritance; and he went out, not knowing where he was going"* (Hebrews 11:8).

To escape the pull and distractions of Ur, Abram had to leave the familiar. Genesis 12:1-3 tells us:

> *Now the LORD said to Abram, "Go forth from your country, and from your relatives and from your father's house, to the land which I will show you; and I will make you a great nation, and I will bless you, and make your name great; and so you shall be a blessing; and I will bless those who bless you, and the one who curses you I will curse. And in you all the families of the earth will be blessed."*

As with Abraham, our journey through times of wilderness relies on growing trust and connection with God.

A little while back I was serving a small church in northern Bedford County of Pennsylvania. I had driven the same route a couple of times each week to minister to this small group of precious people. One particular Sunday, after the morning service, I was driving home and decided to take a left instead of a right turn at a particular intersection. I thought I knew where the road would lead me. Some of the drive seemed familiar as I drove along a beautiful stream. But after half an hour or so, I realized I was totally lost. To make it more complicated, there was no cell service in this wild place so I could not call for direction nor find it with the GPS feature of my cellphone. I was adrift in a sea of trees and forest without a compass or stars to guide me.

I began to grip the steering wheel a bit more tightly as the territory, sprinkled with a few houses, looked less and less familiar. I recall saying something like, "God, I have no idea where I am." In a moment I seemed to hear the Lord say, "I know where you are. You are with Me." I loosened my grip and looked around at the scenery and enjoyed the rest of the drive. (It was only an hour longer than my usual drive.) I was not lost; God knew where I was. God knows where we are in whatever kind of wilderness we may find ourselves.

There are varieties of wilderness, but whatever kind of wilderness we find ourselves, of whatever description, it is a place of separation and preparation.

The Wilderness Is a Place of Quiet and Listening

The Jewish Publication Society translation of Exodus 3:1 reads, *"Moses went to the farthest end of the wilderness."* Wilderness separation is perhaps to the farthest side of the familiar. The wilderness may mean separation from what is familiar, but also separation **to** God. On one hand, our wilderness may be a place where we feel alone—but it can also be a place of an undistracted separation and solitude, and a closeness to God.

The Gospels record Jesus seeking solitude in a wilderness to be alone with the Father more than forty times. Examples of His practice of solitude are found throughout the Gospels: *"But He Himself would often slip away to the wilderness and pray"* (Luke 5:16). *"And it was at this time that He went off to the mountain to pray, and He spent the whole night in prayer to God"* (Luke 6:12). (See also Luke 9:18; Matthew 14:23; John 6:15.) Jesus sought deliberate times of solitude with a greater emphasis on personal devotion to the presence of the Father. The wilderness was a place of separation *to* God not *from* Him.

In that separation and solitude, we are changed. Speaking of the wilderness,

Henri Nouwen writes, "*Solitude is the furnace of transformation. Without solitude, we remain victims of our society and continue to be entangled in the illusions of false self.*"[2] In the wilderness, we become who we truly are.

The wilderness is a place of separation to hear the voice of God. When Jesus was baptized as seen in the gospels, the voice of the Spirit declared, "*This is My beloved Son, in whom I am well- pleased*" (Matthew 3:17). But immediately, this same Spirit who announced His belovedness, led Jesus into the wilderness:

> *Then Jesus was led up by the Spirit into the wilderness to be tempted by the devil. And after He had fasted forty days and forty nights, He then became hungry. And the tempter came and said to Him, "If You are the Son of God, command*

that these stones become bread." But He answered and said, "It is written, 'MAN SHALL NOT LIVE ON BREAD ALONE, BUT ON EVERY WORD THAT PROCEEDS OUT OF THE MOUTH OF GOD'" (Matthew 4:1-4).

The Hebrew word we translate as "wilderness" in the Hebrew Bible is *midbar*, which holds the word *dabar*, meaning to speak. The Old Testament prophet Hosea records, *"Therefore, behold, I will allure her,* ***bring her into the wilderness and speak*** *kindly to her."* Jonathan Cahn writes, "So God brings us to the wilderness that we might hear His voice. Therefore, do not fear or despise the wildernesses of your life, and don't despise His removing of the distractions. Rather embrace it. Draw closer to Him."[3]

It may also seem true to us that God is silent in the wilderness. When God seems to be quiet, we must be even more quiet. The psalmist speaks the heart of God: *"Be still, and know that I am God"* (Psalm 46:10 New King James Version).

The Wilderness Is a Place of Preparation

Most of the people who did great works for the Kingdom of God had times in the wilderness, so much so that we could fill an entire volume with those wilderness experiences. We have already mentioned Abraham who was told by God to leave all that was familiar to him to become a great nation.

Now consider Joseph who was thrown in a pit in the wilderness and sold into slavery by his brothers (Genesis 37:22). Joseph endured the wilderness of slavery as the result of a false accusation by Potiphar's unfaithful wife, which landed him in prison. He endured the indignities of prison only to rise above his captivity to save his family and provide food for an entire nation in time of famine. Joseph became the salvation for his family and an entire nation. (See Genesis 50:20.)

There is a phrase repeated in the account of Joseph: "*The LORD was with Joseph*" (Genesis 39:2,21). The psalmist records the repurposing power of the wilderness, even the wilderness of unjust imprisonment:

> *He sent a man before them, Joseph, who was sold as a slave. They afflicted his feet with fetters, he himself was laid in irons; until the time that his word came to pass,* ***the word of the LORD tested him****. The king sent and*

> *released him, the ruler of peoples, and set him free. He made him lord of his house and ruler over all his possessions* (Psalm 105:17-21).

In this wilderness Joseph was "tested," or perhaps it would be better to say that he was refined. Our times of wilderness remove all the dross of distraction revealing the heart of God. In the wilderness, when we have exhausted our own reason and resources, the repurposing grace of God encompasses us. In a tender moment of reconciliation, Joseph speaks of God's repurposing grace saying, *"As for you, you meant evil against me,* ***but*** *God meant it for good to bring about this present result, to preserve many people alive"* (Genesis 50:20).

Also consider David, the overlooked or forgotten son of Jesse, who learned to defeat the enemies of his flock in the wilderness.

In the simplicity and solitude of the wilderness, David became a *man after God's heart* (see 1 Samuel 13:14) who would decapitate a loudmouthed giant in the name of the Living God and would go on to become the great king of all the tribes of God's people.

Consider Jacob, the lying son of Isaac, who was sent off in fear and disgrace having stolen a blessing from his father, Isaac. Jacob would encounter God in the wilderness of Luz, wrestle with the angel of God, and would become the father of the twelve tribes of Israel. God recounts the story of Israel in the Torah:

> *He [God]* ***found*** *him in a desert land, and in the howling waste of a wilderness; He* ***encircled*** *him, He* ***cared*** *for him, He* ***guarded*** *him as the pupil of His eye. Like an eagle that stirs up its*

> *nest, that* ***hovers*** *over its young,* ***He spread His wings*** *and caught them, He* ***carried*** *them on His pinions* (Deuteronomy 32:11-10).

Consider what God did with Jacob in the wilderness from this passage in Deuteronomy 32. God *found* Jacob, *encircled* or *gathered* him into His arms, *cared* for him, *guarded* him, *hovered* over him, and *carried* him. Put yourself in the place of Jacob and the people of God. God, a carrying God, will do the same for you in the midst of whatever kind of wilderness you are in at this moment.

In the wilderness of whatever kind, the Lord removes us from the familiar, erases the blackboard, and perhaps even confuses our compass to speak to us in terms that defy our present understanding and that draws us closer to His heart. In our wilderness, God increases and we decrease as we depend solely on the presence and power of God moment by moment. In the wilderness, we are emptied so that we can be filled with the presence and purpose of God.

The wilderness of whatever kind can also be a place of preparation to encounter God at a new depth. As we grow quieter, the Spirit of God leads us into something new or tender in His heart as we present ourselves to the Person and heart of God.

The Turn Around

There are a few certainties about the wilderness: 1) you have been in one, 2) you are in one, or 3) you will be in one. Let's take some time to think about these three certainties. Consider times past or present circumstances where you were in a wilderness of unfamiliarity. How did you connect with the heart of God in times of past times of wilderness? As you consider that time now, how was the Lord speaking to you in the wilderness? What did you carry with you out of that wilderness time?

You may be in a wilderness even as you read these words. You are not lost, beloved. The Shepherd knows where you are. He can find you and gather you into His arms—He cares for you—He is guarding you—His Spirit hovers over you even at this moment. Take time in a quiet place to read slowly through Deuteronomy 32:10-11, cited again below. Allow the Spirit to reveal the lost and wandering place in your life. Focus on the words I've bolded in the text. Spend a little time now breathing in those words and experiences.

*He **found** him in a desert land,*

And in the howling waste of a wilderness;

*He **encircled** him, He **cared** for him,*

*He **guarded** him as the pupil of His eye.*

Like an eagle that stirs up its nest,

*That **hovers** over its young,*

*He **spread His wings** and caught them,*

*He **carried** them on His pinions.*

Notes

1. Alan D. Wolfelt, *The Wilderness of Grief: Finding Your Way* (Buchanan, NY: Companion Press, 2010), 13.

2. Henri Nouwen, *The Way of the Heart; The Spirituality of the Desert Fathers and Mothers*, (New York: Harper Collins, 1981), 20.

3. Jonathan Cahn, *The Book of Mysteries* (Lake Mary, FL: Charisma House, 2018), 8.

Chapter 4

The Repurposing of the Wilderness

The angel of the LORD appeared to him in a blazing fire from the midst of a bush; and he looked, and behold, the bush was burning with fire, yet the bush was not consumed. So Moses said, "I must turn aside now and see this marvelous sight, why the bush is not burned up." When the LORD saw that he turned aside to look, God called to him from the midst of the bush and said, "Moses, Moses!" And he said, "Here I am" (Exodus 3:2-4).

Put yourself in the sandals of Moses for a minute. Maybe you are in his sandals right now. What emotions and thoughts must have run through his heart and mind? This encounter on a mountain, often representing a place of solitude and reflection, at the edge of the wilderness took place forty years after Moses fled from Egypt (see Acts 7:30). God had not forgotten Moses. Egypt was out of Moses' system. Moses had gotten married, had a couple sons, and had nothing left but to shepherd the flocks of his father-in-law, Jethro.

What might Moses have thought as he sat alone at night by a campfire resting among the sheep? What thoughts of what might have been replayed in his head as he consumed some meager ration recalling the sumptuous foods of Egypt? I have to believe that as Moses listened to the bleating of sheep and the sound of the wind in the wilderness that there were remnants of disappointments and loss. But God has a long memory. He had not forgotten Moses.

Now as the embers of Moses' life and flight from Egypt were going out, a new flame was ignited in the form of a bush that burned but was not consumed. The far side of the wilderness brought Moses into a face-to-face encounter with the Eternal. The greatest rescue mission in the history of Israel began in this conversation. The man who likely believed his life was over was just beginning a new and powerful chapter. This conversation reveals a process that you and I go through to make sense of the pile of rubble in which we sometimes find ourselves.

One of the benefits of the wilderness and its silence is that it has the effect of preparing us to hear from God if we will turn aside from our own understanding to watch God transform our wilderness into a spring. As the psalmist says, *"He changes a wilderness into a pool of water and a dry land into springs of water"* (Psalm 107:35).

As you read these words, you are immersed in a sea of God's presence. Psalm 139:7 reads: *"Where can I go from Your Spirit? Or where can I flee from Your presence?"* The question is whether we are paying attention to the activity of God around us. Our times in the quiet of the wilderness prepare us for encounters with something new or unexpected, just as Moses encountered the Eternal in the form of a bush that burned yet was not consumed. Moses was not, as far as we know from the text, a follower or seeker of Yahweh. But Yahweh is the Eternal Seeker. Jesus said, *"But an hour is coming, and now is, when the true worshipers will worship the Father in spirit and truth; for such people the Father seeks to be His worshipers"* (John 4:23).

In Exodus 3:2, most English translations cite that *"The angel of the LORD"* appeared to Moses. The Hebrew word here is *malach*, a messenger and manifestation of the presence of God. The word translated LORD, Yahweh, literally means, "I am." Jesus Christ identified with the designation, "I am" seven times in the Gospels:

- "***I am*** the bread of life" John 6:35
- "***I am*** the Light of the world" John 8:12

- "***I am*** the door" John 10:9
- "***I am*** the good shepherd" John 10:11
- "***I am*** the resurrection and the life" John 11:25
- "***I am*** the way, and the truth, and the life" John 14:6
- "***I am*** the vine" John 15:5

In fact, when the guards came to arrest Jesus in the garden of Gethsemane, He deliberately referred to Himself as "I am." (See John 18:8.) As I reflect on this passage I believe the Messenger who appeared to Moses in his wilderness is none other than the pre-incarnate Jesus Christ, the Logos, the express image of the Father. (See Colossians 1:15.) Moses had a face-to-face, presence-to-Presence encounter with the Son of God.

There is a sequence to entering into this new season. Moses looked, then turned aside to see the presence of God. It is important to note that the presence of God was already aflame in the bush before Moses arrived on the scene. And so God is at the edge of our own wilderness if we will open ourselves up to Him. Often we are so mired in our wilderness of circumstance that we cannot lift up our eyes to see the presence of God. Our part in this sequence is to turn aside and look or watch for what God might be doing right in front of us.

To turn aside is to be willing to leave our regular path, opening ourselves to a new chapter in life. Turning aside involves moving in a new direction—finding new purpose and meaning even to the times we have spent in the wilderness. As we turn aside, God begins to repurpose our times of wilderness, trauma, disappointments. His presence is aflame before us as we open ourselves to new possibilities.

The Eternal God responded to Moses' turning aside as he presented himself to God. He had hit bottom and there was nothing left to hold onto. The clutter was gone. When the Lord saw that Moses turned aside to look, God *called* to him from the midst of the bush and said, "Moses, Moses!" So in the midst or at the edge of our wilderness of whatever kind, we see and turn aside, opening ourselves to the Presence of God, and God invites us to go a little further in our relationship with Him. We are cultivating a lifestyle of looking for God even in our times of challenge and unbinding the hand of God in our lives. We open to God; God opens to us.

Moses' response to the calling of God was a simple, *"Here I am"* (Exodus 3:4). This phrase, *"Here I am,"* is *hineniy* in Hebrew and is a presentation of ourselves to the Presence and purpose of God. God called us to where we are when He calls, He is not waiting for some more appropriate time or resolved circumstance; He calls in the middle of it. This simple phase, *"Here I am"* is repeated throughout the Scriptures. When I read this phrase in the Scriptures, I'm expecting something new to be revealed in God. He is inviting us to His ways and His thoughts, which are higher than ours (see Isaiah 55:9).

Am I open? Am I available?

Jesus is the ultimate example of openness to God. One instance is a conversation Jesus has with a Samaritan woman at Jacob's well:

And He had to pass through Samaria. So He came to a city of Samaria called Sychar, near the parcel of ground that Jacob gave to his son Joseph; and Jacob's well was there. So Jesus, being wearied from His journey, was sitting thus by the well. It was about the sixth hour. There came a woman of Samaria to draw water. Jesus said to her, "Give Me a drink" (John 4:4-7).

Here was Jesus, the only begotten Son of God, weary and thirsty at a well called Sychar, which is the same as Shechem in the Old Testament. Shechem was an important location representing a place of separation to God. It was at Shechem that God makes a covenant of faith with Abraham (Genesis 12). At Shechem Joseph was buried. At Shechem the Word of God was read and the covenant with Israel reiterated. Shechem is also between Mount Ebal and Gerizim. One represents the Kingdom of God, the other the world. Therefore, it was a place of separation to God and of decision. This was an encounter of thirst meeting thirst. Jesus went out of His way and His religion to speak with this non-Jewish woman to bring her water to quench an eternal thirst.

Another example is Jesus in John 5 when He heals a man who had laid by the well at Bethesda for thirty-eight years. Of course the religious establishment accused Jesus of coloring outside the lines and breaking the Sabbath, which, by the way, He never did. What is instructive to us is the statement that Jesus makes to the religious folks: *"For this reason the Jews were persecuting Jesus, because He was doing these things on the Sabbath. But He answered them, 'My Father is working until now, and I Myself am working*'" (John 5:16-17). Jesus had to have walked by that location many times, yet on that day He was open to the Father to heal a hopeless man.

But we cannot fulfill the calling and invitation of God in our own strength and understanding.

> *Then He said, "Do not come near here; remove your sandals from your feet, for the place on which you are standing is holy ground." He said also, "I am the God of your father, the God of Abraham, the God of Isaac, and the God of Jacob." Then Moses hid his face, for he was afraid to look at God* (Exodus 3:5-6).

God has further instruction. Moses turned aside to see, then God called, and Moses responded, "Here I am." Now God says, in essence, "Take off your shoes,

Moses." As if to say, "Don't track the world and your understanding into My presence. The Kingdom of God is not Burger King, you can't have it your way." In order for God to repurpose the wilderness, Moses had to relinquish all of the past to Him.

In this intimate encounter, Moses is unsure of himself as God calls Moses into this great mission of deliverance. In that conversation, Moses responds to God's invitation with a question: *"Who am I?"* (Exodus 3:11). Then when God sends Moses back to tell the people of God of his encounter with I AM, he asks God, "What if they don't believe me?" Whereupon God poses the great repurposing question, *"What is in your hand?"* (Exodus 4:2). I can imagine a conversation that could have ensued here.

Moses says, "*What if*...they don't believe that You have *appeared* to me?"

God asks, “Moses, what is in your hand?”

Moses responds, “It’s a stick, just a piece of dead wood.”

I AM responds with another question, “Where did you get that stick, Moses?”

“Just back in the wilderness.”

“Really. Well what do you do with that stick, Moses?

“I use it to protect myself from wild animals. Sometimes I use it as a tool…I mostly use it to lean on. It’s just a stick.”

“Moses, that stick which you see as just a piece of dead wood is all the disappointments you found in your wilderness. It the pain, the loneliness, the hurts. I’m going to repurpose it! Now cast that stick down at My feet. When you do, I am going to transform it and empower it and it will bring Me glory. With that stick in your hand you will destroy the power of Pharaoh. You will bring deliverance to the people of God and take them through all kinds of obstacles, through the Red Sea, through hunger and thirst. Through battles with the enemies of My Kingdom purposes. Your stick is the master stick! That will be the proof I've appeared to you. That's who you are. That's why they will believe you," says I AM.

Beloved of God, the proof of our encounter with I AM is not our perfection; it's His repurposing of our sticks! If we will turn aside to see what He is doing, He will call forth all our past hurts and challenges and repurpose them for His glory and the glory of His Kingdom. We must remove the shoes of our own understanding and operate in the truth of who He is. He is the I

AM. The eternally creative and repurposing God. Those things we present to God can be transformed and empowered as we lay them at His feet and make them our redemptive resumé.

The cross of Christ is the master stick onto which the Master was affixed so cruelly. As the apostle Paul writes, *"May it never be that I would boast, except in the cross of our Lord Jesus Christ, through which the world has been crucified to me, and I to the world"* (Galatians 6:14).

The sticks—the challenges and disappointments and failures that you and I have carried for years—that we may not have seen as valuable can be presented at His feet.

The Turn Around

Let's take inventory. What are some of the sticks you have picked up in the wilderness? What did you learn—what compassion have they worked in your life? How might these sticks be repurposed if you placed them at the feet of I AM?

About the Cover

The picture on the front cover is based on an ancient Japanese art-form called *Kintsugi* where the pieces of broken pottery are put back together using molten gold. The broken and repurposed vessels become precious works of art.

About the Author

Thom Gardner has ministered as a Bible teacher or pastor since 1986, and is now president of Restored Life Ministries, Inc., a ministry dedicated to the spiritual healing and growth of the body of Christ. Dr. Gardner and his wife, Carol, travel internationally to equip leaders throughout the body of Christ by leading retreats and training seminars using his techniques of interactive encounter of the presence of Christ through the Scriptures.

Dr. Gardner holds a Doctor of Ministry focused on Spiritual Formation from Winebrenner Theological Seminary,

Findlay, Ohio, where he has also served as an adjunct professor of Spiritual Formation.

Seminars developed and facilitated include:

- *Restored Life Equipping Seminar*
- *Rewriting Your Life Sentence*
- *Grace at the Table, Marriage Encounters*
- *Seven Things to Tell Your Children*
- *Living the God-Breathed Life*
- *Make Up Your Mind: Moving from Decision to Discernment*
- *Everything That Grows*
- *Becoming the Beloved*
- *The Missing Peace*

- *Seeing the Invisible*

Books

- *Healing the Wounded Heart: Overcoming Obstacles to Intimacy with God*
- *The Healing Journey: An Interactive Guide to Spiritual Wholeness*
- *Relentless Love: Unfolding the Passion, Presence, and Glory of God*
- *Living the God-Breathed Life: An Invitation to Rest at the Table with Jesus*
- *Everything that Grows: Finding Your Rhythm of Spiritual Life in Christ*
- *Growing Up Into Christ: A Study in Integrated Spiritual Formation*

- *Seeing the Invisible: 90 Days of Experiencing the Passion, Presence & Purpose of God*

ECourse

- *Grace at the Table: Overcoming Obstacles in Relationship through Compassion*

www.ingramcontent.com/pod-product-compliance
Lightning Source LLC
Chambersburg PA
CBHW070537030426
42337CB00016B/2242